Very Rare
GLASSWARE
of the Depression Years

Sixth Series
Identification and Values

Gene Florence

COLLECTOR BOOKS
A Division of Schroeder Publishing Co., Inc.

The current values in this book should be used only as a guide. They are not intended to set prices, which vary from one section of the country to another. Auction prices as well as dealer prices vary greatly and are affected by condition as well as demand. Neither the Author nor the Publisher assumes responsibility for any losses that might be incurred as a result of consulting this guide.

Other Books by Gene Florence

On the cover:

Top left — PORTIA Crown Tuscan w/gold decoration #1237 9" vase

Center — MORGAN black w/gold decoration, 10" bud vase

Top right — WILDFLOWER ebony w/gold decoration #648/119, 6" candelabrum

Bottom right — MOONDROPS "Rocket" tumbler

Bottom left — GLORIA Crown Tuscan w/gold decoration #1312 footed cigarette box

COLLECTOR BOOKS
P.O. Box 3009
Paducah, KY 42002-3009

Gene Florence
P.O. Box 22186
Lexington, KY 40522

Contents

Gene Florence, Jr., born in Lexington in 1944, graduated from the University of Kentucky where he held a double major in mathematics and English.

Mr. Florence has been interested in "collecting" since childhood, beginning with baseball cards and progressing through comic books, coins, bottles, and finally, glassware. He first became interested in Depression glassware after purchasing an entire set of Sharon dinnerware for $5.00 at a garage sale.

He has written several books on glassware: The Collector's Encyclopedia of Depression Glass in its thirteenth edition; Kitchen Glassware of the Depression Years, in its fifth edition with updated values; four editions of Collectible Glassware from the 40's, 50's, 60's. . .; Elegant Glassware of the Depression Era, in its eighth edition; The Collector's Encyclopedia of Occupied Japan, Volumes I, II, III, IV, V and Price Guide Update Series 1-5; Very Rare Glassware of the Depression Years, Volumes I, II, III, IV, V, and VI; Stemware Identification and the Pocket Guide to Depression Glass, now in its eleventh edition. His latest book, Anchor Hocking's Fire-King and More is receiving enthusiastic reviews. A Pattern Identification guide will be issued about the time of this book's release. He also authored six editions of a baseball book and three editions of The Collector's Encyclopedia of Akro Agate, that are now out of print, as well as a book on Degenhart Glass for that museum.

Mr. Florence sells glassware at Depression Glass shows throughout the country as well as through his web page (http://www.geneflorence.com).

If you know of rare or unusual pieces of glassware in the patterns shown in his books, you may write him at Box 22186, Lexington, KY 40522, or at Box 64, Astatula, FL 34705. If you would like a reply, you must enclose a SASE (self-addressed, stamped envelope) – and be patient. Very little mail is answered between Christmas and the middle of May due to his writing, research, and travel schedule. He spends many hours answering letters when time and circumstances permit which is often on plane trips or in motel rooms across the country. Remember that SASE! He does not open mail. Most letters without SASE are never seen by him!

Foreword

The acceptance of my five earlier editions of Very Rare Glassware of the Depression Years books has led to this sixth and very possibly, last one. Rare glassware continues to be found, but publishing economics make specialized books such as this "iffy" as to the "bottom line" – money. Books have to sell well enough to justify their existence and these rare books have reached the point that they hardly warrant the time plus the publishing costs. Actually, I had some doubts that there was a market for the first one, but I was proved wrong when it was reprinted two or three times! (By the way, a limited, leather bound copy of that first edition recently sold for $125.00 on the Internet!) The success of the first book led to the next four which have done all right, but not as well as my other books on glass. My regret is that most of the type of pieces pictured in these books will not be shown so vividly in my regular books due to lack of space!

Books have to sell in the bookstores, today, to be profitable; and unfortunately, most bookstores do not stock this series of books! If it were to be picked up by a chain or collectors asked for it, there could be another one down the road; but right now, that is unlikely. For all you who love these books and have faithfully supported them over the years, I want to say a heartfelt thanks!

Photographs for this book were taken over a two-year period. As I found rare items, I had them photographed. Often, I borrowed an item, so I did not have to buy it. Several dealers have been gracious in sending me rare glassware they found before they offered it for sale. These "extra" finds really added to the scope of the book! Hopefully, you will appreciate all our efforts in putting this sixth book on rare Depression era glassware together. I further hope the entire series has helped you spot some rare glass. Enjoy!

Acknowledgments

First of all, let me acknowledge that I really value all the enlightenment dealers, readers, and collectors have provided through their writing, calling, e-mailing, and talking to me at various shows around the country! Thanks, too, for carrying those newly discovered pieces to shows for corroboration and for sending measurements and photographs supporting new findings! A picture being worth a thousand words has never been more true than in authenticating an unknown piece. (If you have trouble photographing glass, take it outside in natural light, place the glass on a neutral surface {concrete works}, and ignore the camera flash attachment. A bright, cloudy day is preferred.) Please enclose a SASE (self-addressed stamped envelope) that is large enough to send back your pictures, if you wish them returned.

Many collectors and friends in the business have loaned their rare glassware for photographs for this book, and each is herein gratefully acknowledged with the items pictured. Dick and Pat Spencer also helped by gathering other collectors' treasures and transporting them for photography as well as lending their own pieces. I would like to especially thank Dan Tucker and Lorrie Kitchen for the numerous pieces they have mailed directly to the photography studio! Lynn Welker arranged for glassware to be borrowed from the Cambridge Museum and Marianne Jackson and Barbara Wolfe of Anchor Hocking allowed me to borrow items from the morgue. Without these special people, my job would be much more difficult!

An affirmation is always due family. Cathy, my life partner, has worked many long hours as chief editor, critic, and proofreader. This time, she has also juggled helping paint and decorate two houses (old and new) for Chad and Rebecca while helping me on my books. Marc, my younger son, has overseen shipping book orders and operating my web page (http://www.geneflorence.com) along with working noon until nine each day. So far, I have not had time to surf the web myself! Keeping these books current takes more of my time than I care to admit or you will ever imagine!

Thanks, too, to Cathy's folks, Charles and Sibyl, who helped sort and pack glass for photography. Both Charles and Sibyl have helped us at recent glass shows when we have suffered some health or accident problems. (I believe they like Florida in January and February!) It seems the older we get, the more pieces that operate poorly or not at all. Blood sugar has been my major headache, while Cathy keeps developing hand nerve problems; so movement causes pain. I'm very grateful to family who try to keep everything under control at home while we travel. I truly couldn't manage all this without their constant support.

Photographs for this book were created by Richard Walker of New York and Charley Lynch of Collector Books. They both managed multiple photographs during one six-day session plus numerous other sessions of photographing glass. Glass arranging, unpacking, sorting, carting, and repacking were accomplished by Jane White, Zibbie Walker, Dick and Pat Spencer, and Cathy Florence. Van loading and unloading were facilitated by Billy Schroeder and some of Collector Books' shipping crew.

Thank you for your continued loyalty through these six editions depicting the rarest Depression era glassware!

AKRO AGATE COMPANY 1911–1951

Akro Agate Company was founded in Akron, Ohio, in 1911. Originally, they produced marbles and games there until, for financial reasons, the company moved to Clarksburg, West Virginia, in 1914. Clarksburg offered quality sand as well as a vast supply of cheap natural gas. These were the two most needed materials for making glass marbles.

World War I helped to establish the Akro Agate Company as a major force in the marble making industry. Until that war, the importing of marbles from Germany had kept Akro Agate a fledgling business. With the demise of European competition due to the war, Akro Agate was able to fortify itself in the field of marble making to the point that by the Depression years, they manufactured seventy-five percent of the marbles made in the United States.

A competitor, Master Marbles, cut into Akro's business when it hired some of the machine designers working at Akro. (Those machines had never been patented to keep others from getting information on making their own!) Today, that is seen as a fortuitous turning point for collectors. Because of losing business in the marble industry, Akro began making other objects from the same material. Flower pots, planters, and other utility items were made. After the Westite Glass Company burned in 1936, Akro obtained their moulds and made a strong line of these items that prospered until World War II. During the latter half of the 1930s, they made children's doll dishes, tobacco accessory items (ashtrays, match holders, powder jars, etc.) and other utilitarian items. The doll or "play" dishes became a major line when "metal" play dishes disappeared since that material was needed for the machines of war. As Akro Agate had prospered during WWI, they again prospered because of WWII.

Paradoxically, the fate of this little company was sealed at the end of the war by the introduction of plastic doll dishes and increased competition from Japan. In 1951, Akro Agate was sold to Clarksburg Glass Company; and today, collectors search for that elusive trademark (crow flying through the letter A). Akro was a shortened form of "as a crow."

Author's Collection

COCA-COLA® ashtray – rare item

HAMILTON SAFETY TRAY-LITE

ANCHOR HOCKING GLASS COMPANY 1905 to Date

Anchor Hocking was created in 1937 from a merger of Hocking Glass Company and Anchor Container Corporation. Several employees at Anchor Hocking have gone out of their way to help me in my research in the 27 years I have been writing. Anchor Hocking loaned me items from their morgue to be pictured for collectors to see. They have also been at pains to protect the collectibility of their older products by making noticeable changes in any similar reissued wares. Some companies have long since folded, but Anchor Hocking is still meeting consumers' needs!

You can see many more of Anchor Hocking's Fire-King morgue pieces in my Anchor Hocking's Fire-King and More book. Morgue items are not priced unless there have been similar items found outside that storage area.

Author's Collection

BLOCK OPTIC yellow grill plate – rare item
Occasionally, these are found in crystal, but are rare in green or yellow.

CAMEO crystal cocktail shaker – rare item
Several crystal ones have been seen over the years, but none have been found in green.
This one came from the family of a former employee of Hocking.

From the collection of Dan Tucker and Lorrie Kitchen

CAMEO crystal ice bucket – rare color

From the collection of Harold and Susan Watson

COLONIAL pink tab handled berry – rare item

Morgue

CORONATION green 4¼" tab handled berry – rare item

Author's Collection

CORONATION pink 4¼" berry (no handles) – rare item

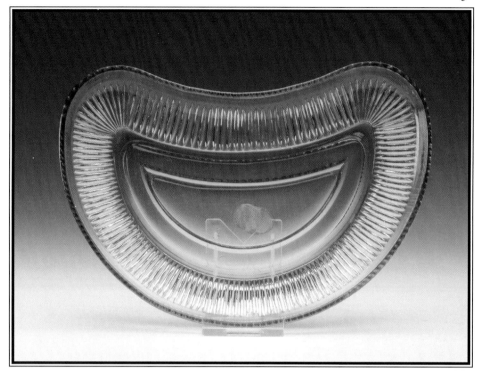

CORONATION pink 7½" crescent salad plate – rare item, one-of-a-kind

FIRE-KING DINNERWARE "PHILBE" blue platter – rare item

From the collection of Earl and Beverly Hines

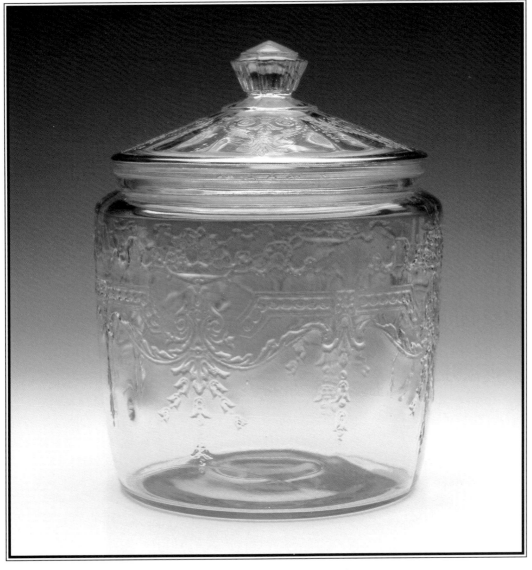

FIRE-KING DINNERWARE "PHILBE" blue cookie jar – rare item

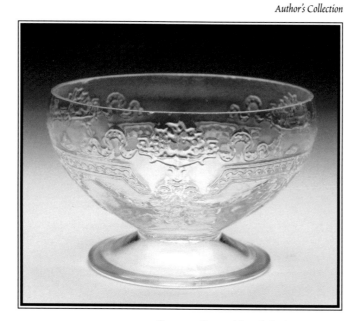

FIRE-KING DINNERWARE "PHILBE" crystal footed sherbet – rare item

FIRE-KING DINNERWARE "PHILBE" green 4¾" tall sherbet – rare item

Morgue Collection

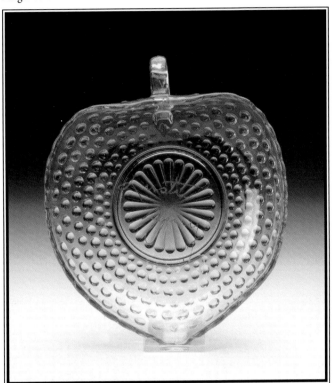

HOBNAIL *Lilac heart bonbon – rare color*
This piece is usually seen in Moonstone, but this color was named Lilac according to labels found on pieces at the factory.

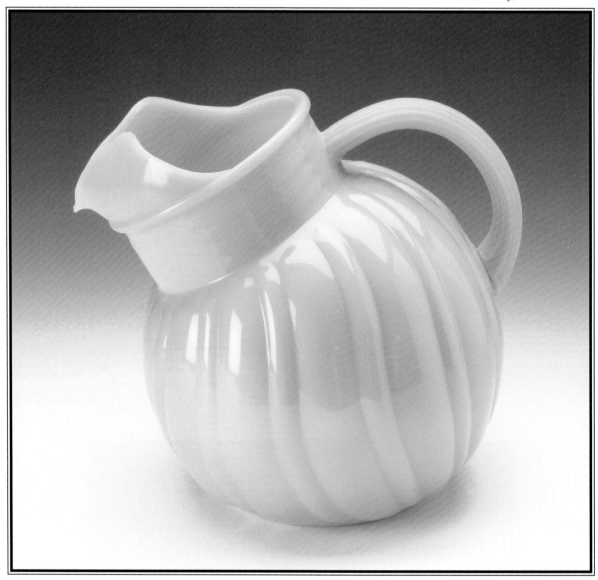

FIRE-KING Jade-ite Swirl 80 oz. pitcher – rare color

From the collection of Molly Allen

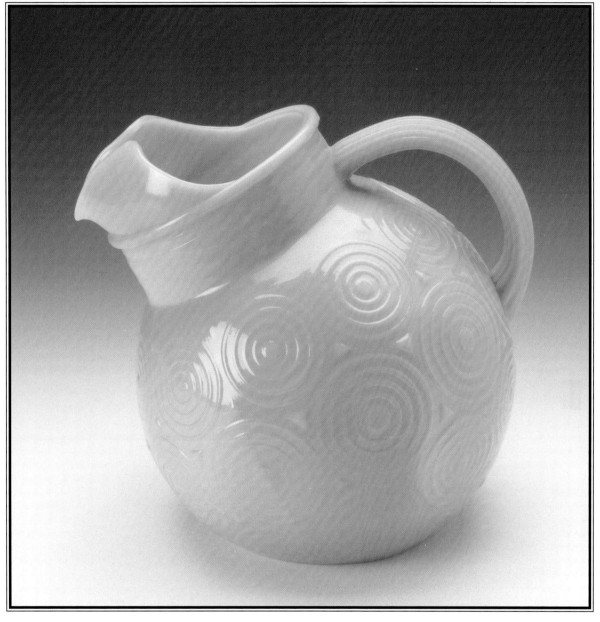

FIRE-KING Jade-ite Target 80 oz. pitcher – rare color

FIRE-KING Jade-ite Kimberly mug – rare color

MANHATTAN Royal Ruby 4" ashtray – rare color

From the collection of Geri Jackson

MANHATTAN ivory 80 oz. pitcher – rare color

MAYFAIR crystal cream soup – rare color, one-of-a-kind

MAYFAIR yellow closed handle platter – rare item

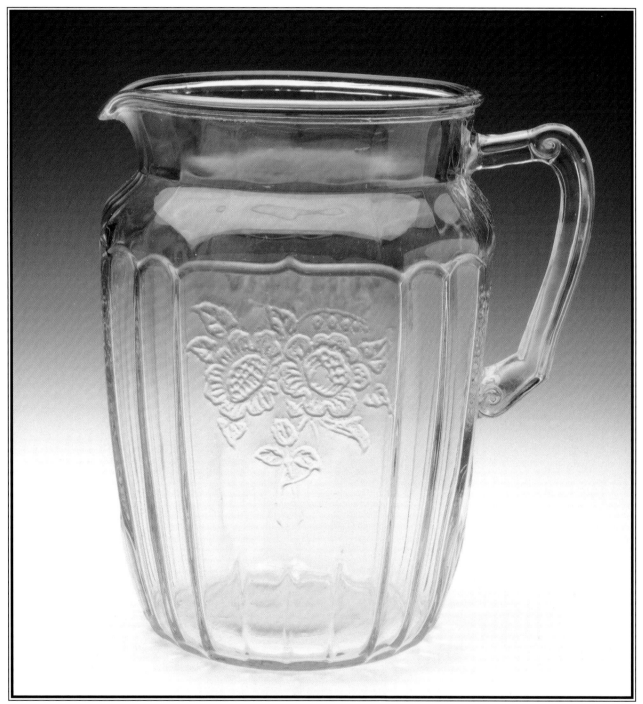

MAYFAIR green 60 oz. pitcher – rare color
Only a couple of green pitchers have been found in this size.

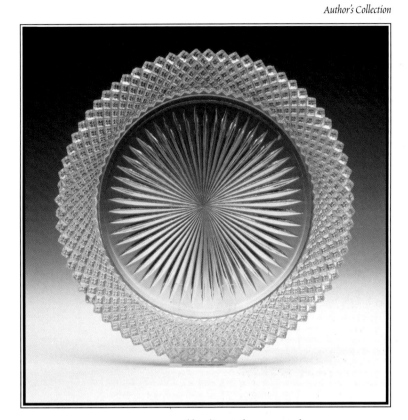

MISS AMERICA blue dinner plate – rare color

MISS AMERICA green shaker – rare color
These were reproduced in the middle 1970s and only a few originals have been seen.

From the collection of Dr. Bob Schmidgalt

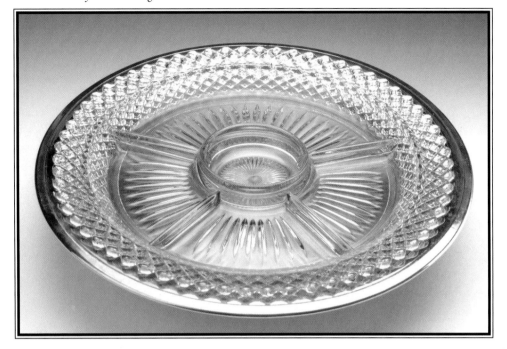

MISS AMERICA *pink, 5-part relish or lazy susan – rare color*
Although these are regularly seen in crystal, only a few have been discovered in pink.

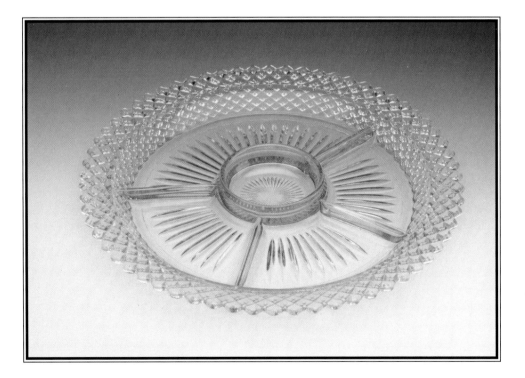

MOONSTONE yellow opalescent sherbet – rare color, one-of-a-kind

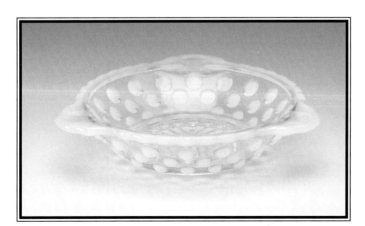

MOONSTONE opalescent 4" ashtray – rare item, one-of-a-kind

Morgue

MOONSTONE opalescent 11⅛" ruffled plate – rare item, one-of-a-kind

Author's Collection

MOONSTONE opalescent 5", 10 oz. tumbler – rare item

MOONSTONE green opalescent sherbet – rare color, one-of-a-kind

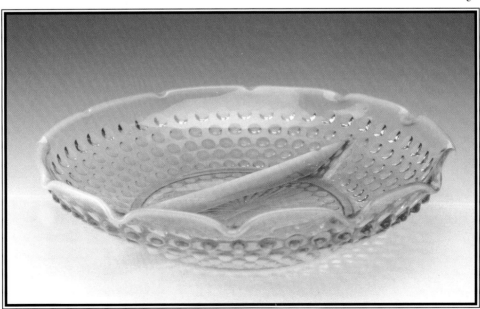

MOONSTONE pink opalescent 7½" divided, crimped bowl – rare color, one-of-a-kind

Morgue

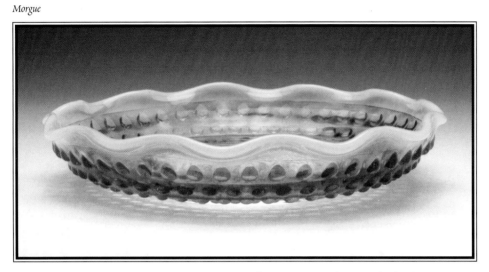

MOONSTONE pink opalescent 7¾" ruffled bowl – rare color, one-of-a-kind

Author's Collection

MOONSTONE red flashed 7¾" bowl – rare color
This bowl and the bowl pictured at top of the next page were found in a flea market in Virginia last year.

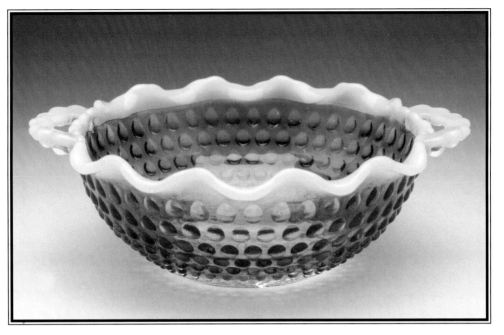

MOONSTONE red flashed two-handled ruffled bowl – rare color and item
Evidently, the candy bottom was used to make this ruffled bowl, but I had never seen the candy bottom ruffled before I found this one.

MOONSTONE yellow opalescent cup and saucer – rare color, one-of-a-kind

Author's Collection

OLD COLONY *pink opalescent 7¾" bowl – rare color*
This bowl was found in the Lancaster, Ohio, area near the factory.

From the collection of Beckye Richardson

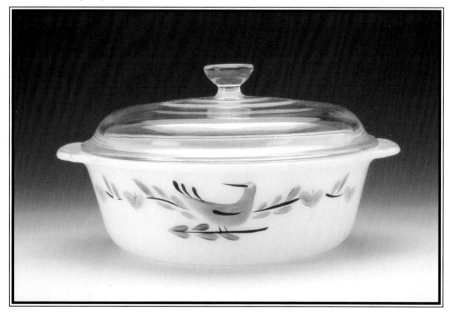

OVENWARE *Distlefink 1½ qt. casserole – rare decoration*

From the collection of Bob and Nancy Cosner

OVENWARE Jade-ite 2 qt. casserole – rare color

From the collection of Molly Allen

OVENWARE Jade-ite gravy or sauce boat – rare color

From the collection of Kenn and Margaret Whitmyer

OVENWARE *Sapphire Blue dry measure – rare item*
Note that this is like an eight-ounce measuring cup without the spout.

Author's Collection

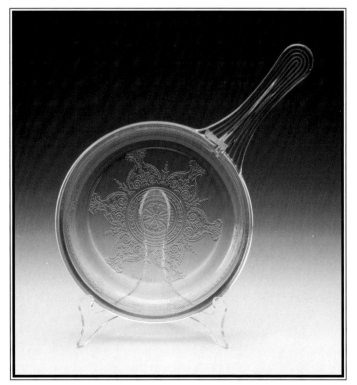

OVENWARE *Sapphire Blue skillet – rare item*
I understand that the handles broke from these skillets too easily, so they were never released for sale.

PRIMROSE vintage 10" footed fruit bowl – rare item

Author's Collection

PRIMROSE Napco vase – rare item

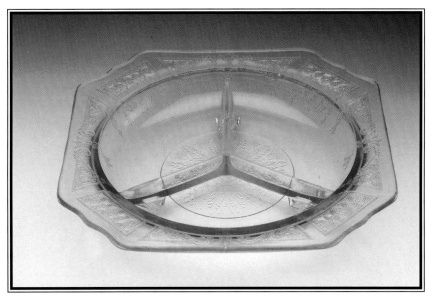

PRINCESS blue 8¾", 3-part, 3-footed relish – rare color and item
A pink relish without the dividers was pictured in the fourth edition of Very Rare Glassware of the Depression Years.

PRINCESS blue 9½" dinner plate – rare color
A publication that "specializes" in reproductions listed this piece as a reproduction. They should check with people who specialize in the field before they jump off the bridge and print erroneous information.

Morgue

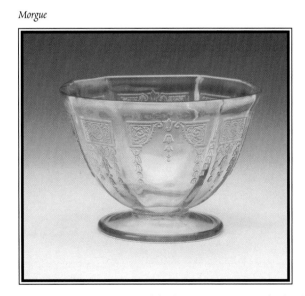

PRINCESS green, non-stemmed sherbet – rare item, one-of-a-kind

QUEEN MARY blue salad plate – rare color

QUEEN MARY pink footed creamer and sugar – rare items

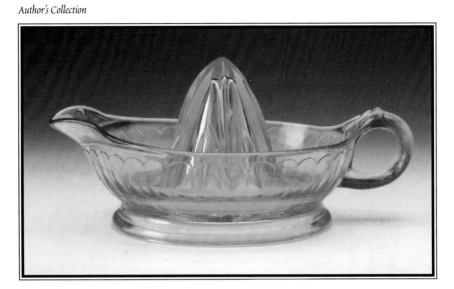

REAMER blue "Mayfair" color – rare color

RING blue cup and saucer – rare color

RING yellow 7¼" goblet — rare color
This is the only piece of yellow Ring I have ever seen!

Morgue

SHEAVES of WHEAT yellow cup – rare color, one-of-a-kind

Author's Collection

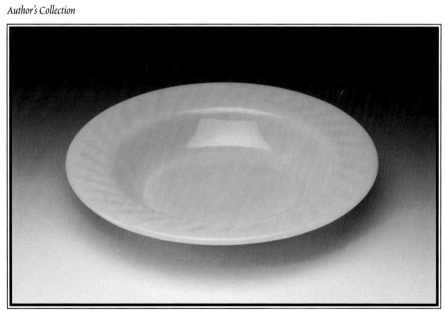

SWIRL Azure-ite flanged soup – rare item

WATERFORD crystal 7¾" wide by 2" high – rare item, one-of-a-kind

CAMBRIDGE GLASS COMPANY 1902–1958

The Cambridge Glass Company was started in Cambridge, Ohio, in 1902. Glass was made there until 1958, except for a short period in 1954 to 1955 when the plant was closed. Today, there is a National Cambridge Collectors Club. A Cambridge Museum is operated by that club and located on Rt. 40E in Cambridge, Ohio.

The glass photographed in this section represents the patterns made during the 1930s to the 1950s that are most collected today. Collectors of Cambridge glass began collecting the glass by colors and decorations that were distinctly Cambridge. However, as more and more Depression glass collectors started to notice the finer handmade glassware from Cambridge, dinnerware lines and sets began to be gathered. Thus, a new standard of collecting was created and the prices started rising.

If you are interested in joining the National Cambridge Collectors Club, their address is:
National Cambridge Collectors, Inc.,
P.O. Box 416GF,
Cambridge, Ohio 43275
(Dues are $17.00 a year.)

The following pages show some of the rarest pieces of Cambridge known in the dinnerware lines, with emphasis on color rarities as well as unusual pieces.

Author's Collection

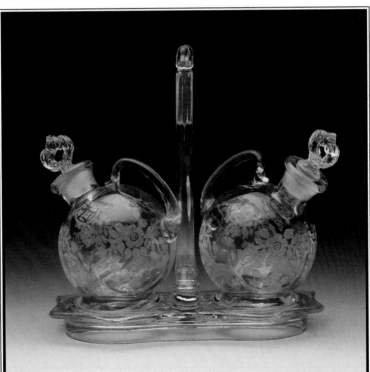

APPLE BLOSSOM Heatherbloom 3400/96 oil and vinegar set – rare color

APPLE BLOSSOM ebony vase w/white gold decoration – rare color

Cambridge Glass Company

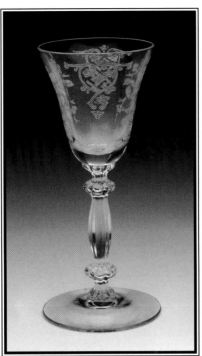

APPLE BLOSSOM blue #3135 4" cordial – rare color

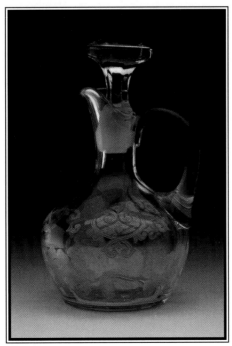

APPLE BLOSSOM blue #193, 6 oz. oil bottle – rare color and item

APPLE BLOSSOM blue ice bucket – rare color

APPLE BLOSSOM Peach Blo #3400 butter dish – rare color

CANDLELIGHT crystal #3400 butter dish – rare item

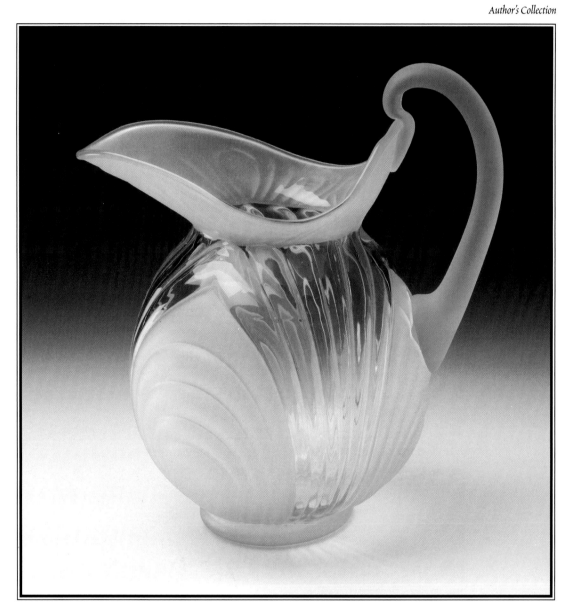

CAPRICE blue Alpine Doulton pitcher – rare item

From the collection of Dan Tucker and Lorrie Kitchen

CAPRICE Peach Blo 80 oz. ball jug – rare color

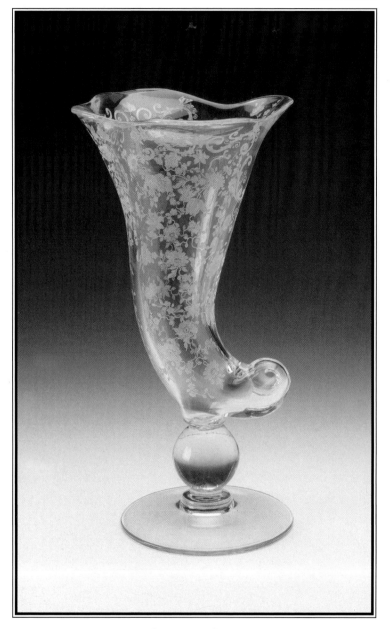

CHANTILLY crystal #3900/575 10″ cornucopia vase – rare item

Author's Collection

CHANTILLY crystal #75 54 oz. pitcher – rare item

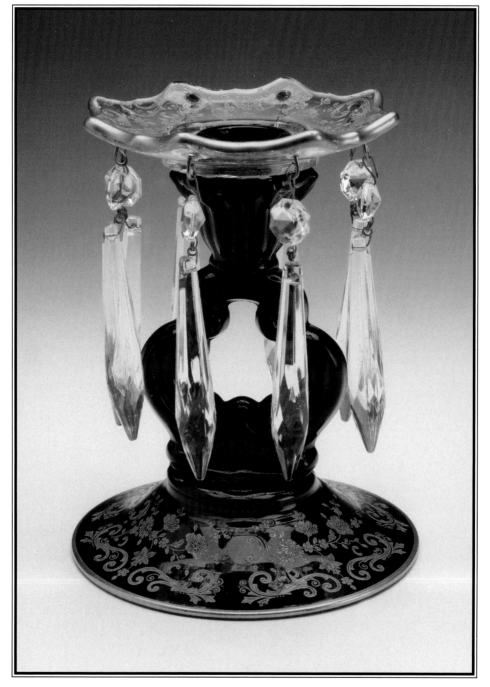

CHANTILLY ebony w/gold decoration #648/119, 6" candelabrum – rare color

Author's Collection

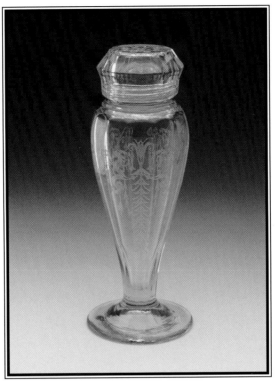

CLEO Willow Blue #813 sugar sifter and #816 ewer creamer – rare items and color

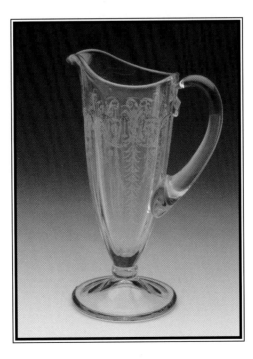

From the collection of Dennis Bialek

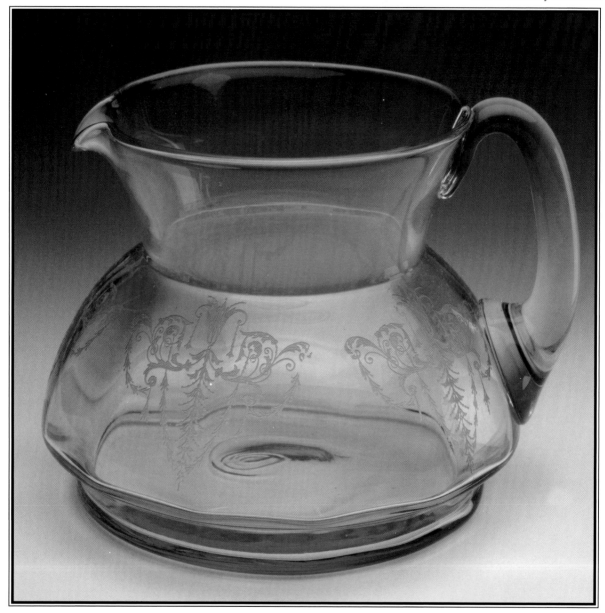

CLEO Willow Blue #955 62 oz. pitcher – rare color

Author's Collection

DIANE amber decanter set – rare set

DIANE crystal #3011 Statuesque cigarette box – rare item

Author's Collection

DIANE gold Krystol #1176 dinner plate – rare color

ELAINE crystal #3500 6″ ram's head candy – rare item

ELAINE crystal #485 9½″ crescent salad plate – rare item

From the collection of Dick and Pat Spencer

ELAINE amethyst frosted goblet – rare color

From the collection of Dick and Pat Spencer

ELAINE crystal frosted goblet – rare color

From the collection of Dick and Pat Spencer

ELAINE emerald frosted goblet – rare color

ELAINE Willow Blue #3500/26 12" fruit basket ram's head bowl – rare color

From the collection of Lynn Welker

EVERGLADE Carmen 6" double candle w/epergnes – rare color

GLORIA Crown Tuscan w/gold decoration #1312 footed cigarette box – rare color

GLORIA Peach Blo #3130 4⅜" cordial – rare color

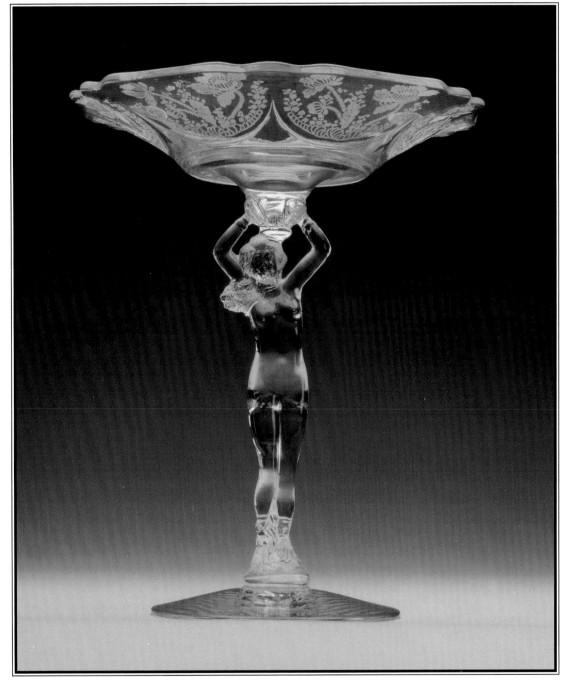

GLORIA gold Krystol 9" #3011 Statuesque comport – rare item

Author's Collection

GLORIA Willow Blue #3130 9″ comport – rare color

MT. VERNON emerald green (dark) #77 5½", two-handled comport – rare color

PORTIA Carmen gold encrusted sherbet and sherbet plate – rare color

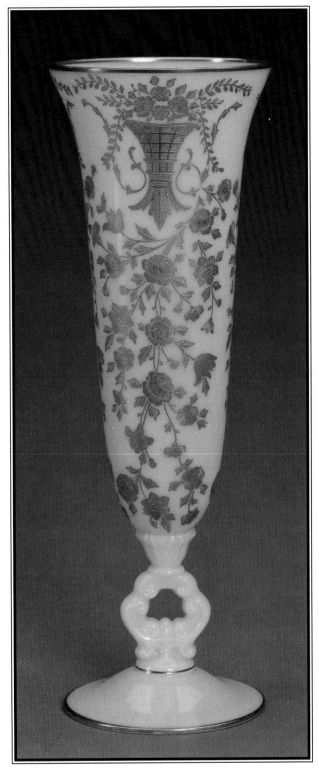

PORTIA Crown Tuscan w/gold decoration #1237 9" vase – rare color

PORTIA crystal #170 13" Martha cake plate – rare item

PORTIA Heatherbloom #3400/1180 5¼" two-handled bonbon – rare color

ROSE POINT crystal #3400/77 shakers w/Ebony tops – rare color

ROSE POINT crystal #1470 ball shaker w/Ebony base – rare color

Bottom left: ROSE POINT crystal #498 2 oz. bar tumbler – rare item
Bottom right: ROSE POINT crystal #321 2 oz. sham to 1½ oz. bar tumbler – rare item

ROSE POINT crystal #1055 32 oz. Weiss beer goblet w/gold — rare item

From the collection of Lynn Welker

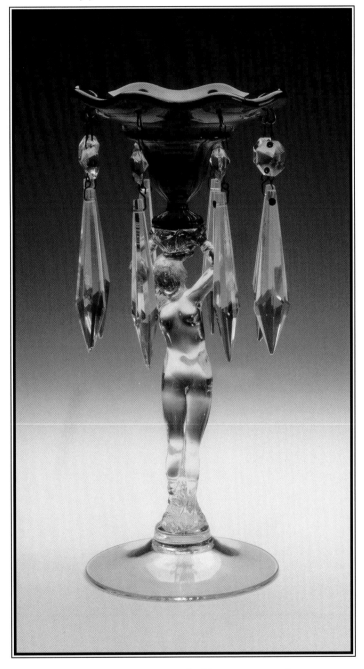

STATUESQUE #3011 candlestick, Carmen – rare item

STATUESQUE #3011 cigarette holder, Mocha – rare color

From the collection of Lynn Welker

STATUESQUE #3011 claret, Smoke Crackle – rare color

STATUESQUE #3011 comport, Crown Tuscan – rare color

From the collection of Lynn Welker

STATUESQUE #3011 comport, Moonlight Blue – rare color
This is the only known Moonlight Blue comport!

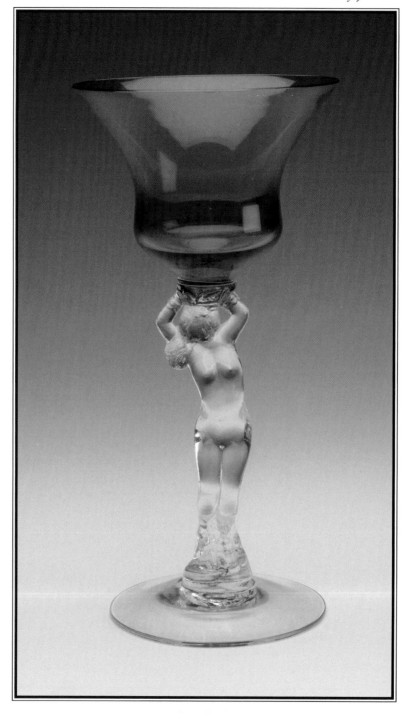

STATUESQUE #3011 tulip cocktail #3126 emerald – rare item

WILDFLOWER crystal #119 7" basket – rare item

WILDFLOWER crystal #1066 oval cigarette holder – rare item

WILDFLOWER crystal Pristine 575 cornucopia vase – rare item

WILDFLOWER ebony w/gold decoration #648/119, 6" candelabrum – rare color

CENTRAL GLASS WORKS 1896–1939

This glass company dates back to the end of the Civil War, but did not become Central Glass Works until 1896. The Morgan pattern depicted here is a new entry in the seventh edition of my *Elegant Glassware of the Depression Era*.

Morgan was designed in 1920 by Joseph O. Balda, who was better known for his Heisey designs. The pattern reputedly was adopted for use in the Governor's Mansion by a West Virginia governing family named Morgan. Someone at the company, in the interest of furthering this marketing coup, named the pattern Morgan.

Author's Collection

MORGAN pink ice tub – rare item

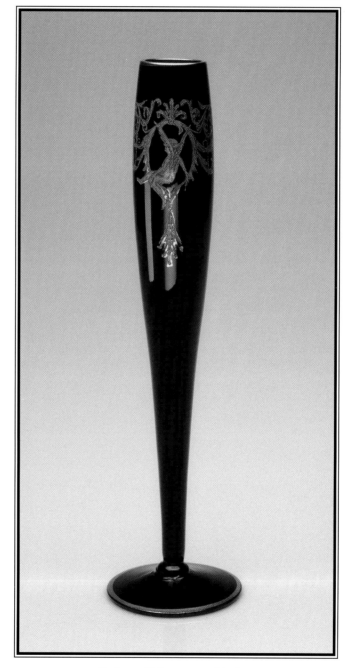

MORGAN black w/gold decoration, 10" bud vase – rare item

MORGAN green 10″ vase w/ruffled top in holder – rare item

CONSOLIDATED LAMP & GLASS COMPANY 1894–1939

Consolidated may be better known for their lamps than for their glassware. Their glassware designs were very different from the norm. Today, collectors really fit into two categories when it comes to Consolidated Glassware. They have an immense love for it or they say, "Get it out of my sight!"

Since the introduction of Ruba Rombic in my last Elegant book, several accumulations have been sold. Prices have settled down after a few years of very rapid rises. Several readers have written saying that they have been unable to sell pieces of Ruba Rombic. It is a very specialized market, and not all areas of the country have collectors willing to pay retail price.

RUBA ROMBIC black 9" vase – experimental item
Only a couple of black pieces have ever been seen in Ruba Rombic!

From the collection of Kevin Kiley

RUBA ROMBIC lilac 3½" ashtray – rare item

From the collection of Kevin Kiley

RUBA ROMBIC Smokey Topaz 3" almond – rare item

RUBA ROMBIC Smokey Topaz 7", 15 oz., ftd. tumbler – rare item
This size tumbler is rarely found in any color.

Author's Collection

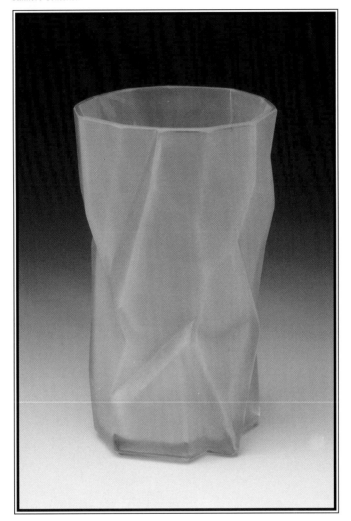

RUBA ROMBIC Jade 12 oz. flat tumbler – rare color

DUNCAN & MILLER GLASS COMPANY 1893–1955

The new Duncan Miller Glass Company was incorporated in 1900 after beginning as the Duncan Glass Company in Pittsburgh and moving to Washington, Pennsylvania, in 1893. Although Duncan's glassware was not as widely distributed as some others, there are many collectors seeking it today.

The patterns made during and shortly after the Depression years are in demand with collectors. One of the more popular patterns is the Caribbean pattern made from 1936 until 1955. Although blue is the desired color, there are also those wanting the crystal.

CANTERBURY ruby 10" oval bowl – rare color

CARIBBEAN blue 6" vase w/frog – rare items
This vase was made by folding down the top edge of a tumbler, but the frog was designed to fit so closely that it is
difficult to remove without turning over the vase. Evidently, this was a short-lived production item and highly sought today.

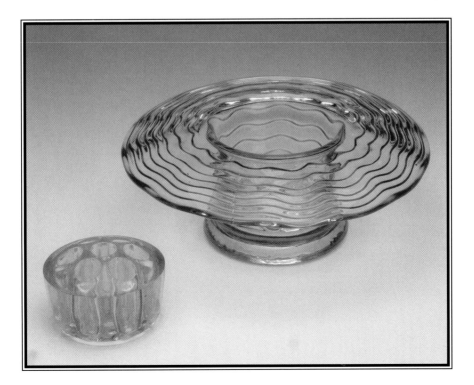

FEDERAL GLASS COMPANY 1900–1984

Federal Glass Company was founded in Columbus, Ohio, and really prospered during the Depression with its dinnerware sets of Madrid, Patrician, Sharon, and Parrot in colors of pink, blue, green, and an amber known as "Golden Glo."

Federal became the first major company to reproduce a pattern from the Depression era with each piece marked. This "Recollection" pattern was copied from the original Madrid, issued in 1976 for the Bicentennial and marked with '76 on each piece. These moulds were later sold to Indiana Glass Company and the '76 removed. Today, Indiana still makes this "Madrid-like" pattern in several colors and in pieces that were not made during the Depression era.

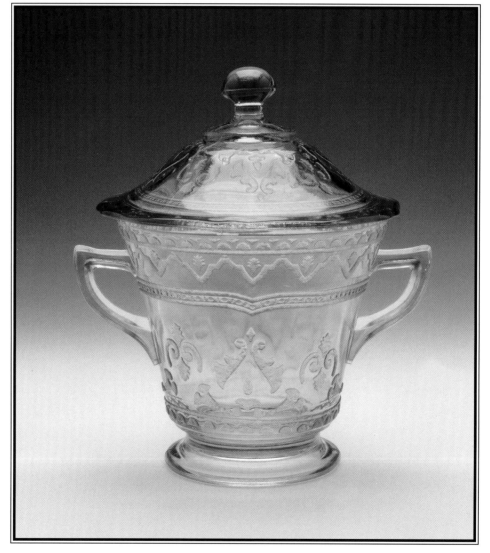

PATRICIAN amber sugar lid – rare item
Look closely at the knob. It is shaped like a Madrid knob and not pointed as the normally found Patrician lid.

From the collection of Bob and Nancy Cosner

SHARON pink footed vase – rare item
One of these surfaced in the mid 1970s and this is the second one known.
It was found about 50 miles from the site of the original Federal Glass Company factory.

FOSTORIA GLASS COMPANY 1887–1986

Fostoria Glass Company survived almost a century! Those years included a major move from Fostoria, Ohio, to Moundsville, West Virginia, in the early days. Lancaster Colony bought Fostoria in the early 1980s, but the glassware in the morgue at the factory was sold as late as December 1986.

The American pattern, first begun in 1915, was one of the longest made patterns in U.S. glassmaking history! Lancaster Colony is continuing to make pieces available in this pattern through Indiana Glass Company and Dalzell Viking Glass Company.

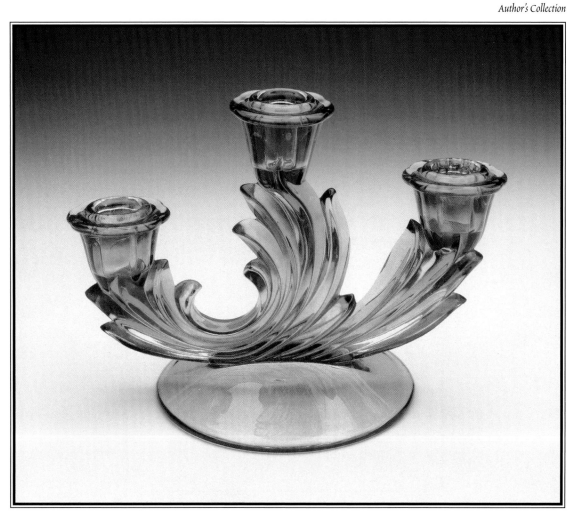

BAROQUE amber 6" three-lite candlestick – rare color

Author's Collection

AMERICAN iridescent 8" vase – rare color

BAROQUE pink 12" flared bowl – rare color
Since there is a console bowl, who has the candlesticks to match?

CENTURY *pink candlestick – rare color*

CHINTZ crystal syrup #2586 sani-cut – rare item

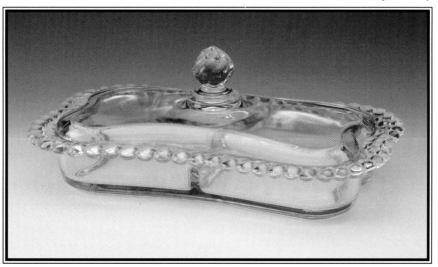

COLONY crystal divided box – rare item

From the collection of Dick and Pat Spencer

HERMITAGE Wisteria #2449, 3-pint pitcher – rare color

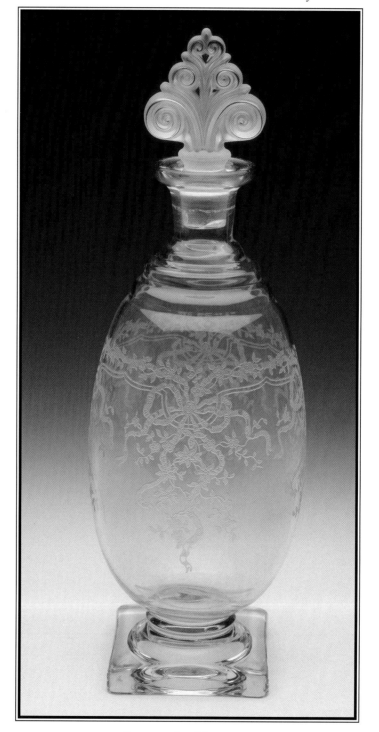

JUNE yellow #4020 footed decanter – rare item

NAVARRE crystal finger bowl – rare item
This finger bowl has never been seen by many Navarre collectors.

ROYAL amber butter dish – rare item

HAZEL-ATLAS GLASS COMPANY 1902–1956

Hazel-Atlas was formed from the merger of Hazel Glass Company and Atlas Glass and Metal Company in 1902. Containers and tumblers were their main wares manufactured until the Depression years. In the 1930s, starting with kitchenware items such as colored mixing bowls, they quickly branched into dinnerware patterns.

The Shirley Temple bowl, mug, and milk pitcher that are recognized by almost everyone were made by Hazel-Atlas. Sets of Royal Lace and Moderntone in Ritz Blue (cobalt) were advertised together for the same price: 44 pieces for $2.99! There is a huge price disparity between those patterns today.

In recent years, it has been the kitchenware and children's sets made by Hazel-Atlas that have come to the forefront. Collectors have eagerly gathered cobalt blue and pink sets of Criss Cross, as well as reamers and measuring cups.

COLONIAL BLOCK green 5¼", 5 oz. ftd. juice – rare item
I found two of these in an antique mall in Ohio last year. It continues to amaze me that unknown pieces in major patterns are still being unearthed.

From the collection of Dan Tucker and Lorrie Kitchen

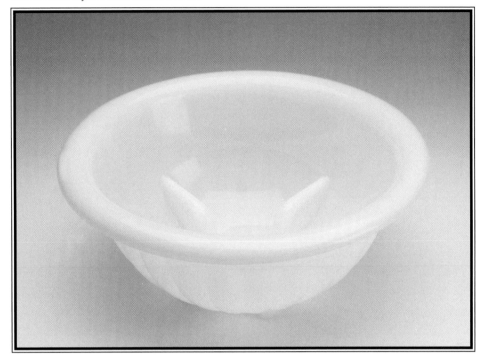

KITCHEN *white utility bowl with dividers – rare item*
If anyone knows the purpose for the dividers in this bowl, let me know. I'm sure there is a purpose, but right now it remains a mystery.

A.H. HEISEY & COMPANY 1896–1957

A.H. Heisey & Company opened its door in 1896. Their handsome pressed glassware was a success. In fact, the innovative idea of advertising glassware in national publications is attributed to Heisey. Glass was made continuously at the plant site in Newark, Ohio, until 1957. As with Cambridge, the glassware made in the 1930s to 1950s is the most collectible today.

One of the most difficult problems facing new collectors comes from the fact that the Heisey moulds were bought by Imperial in 1958, and many pieces were made at that plant until its demise in 1984. New collectors have to learn the Imperial colors because some of these pieces made by Imperial are similar to rare Heisey colors. Crystal pieces are more difficult to distinguish and collectors are beginning to accept this fact. Almost all of those Heisey/Imperial moulds were repurchased by the Heisey Collectors of America, Inc. and are now back in Newark, Ohio.

From the collection of Dick and Pat Spencer

CRYSTOLITE Dawn 12" gardenia bowl – rare color

CRYSTOLITE crystal dresser set – rare set

LODESTAR Dawn double candle – rare item

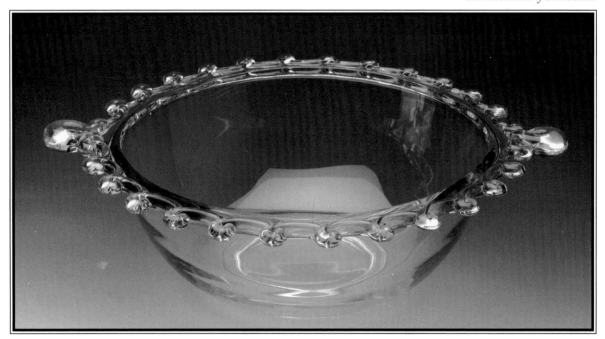

LARIAT crystal 12" handled bowl – rare item

PLANTATION crystal candy dish – rare item

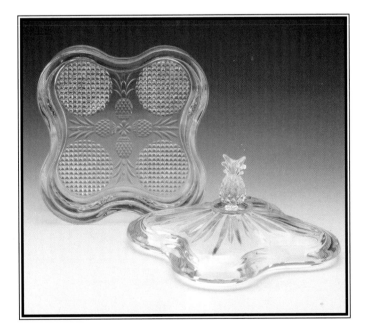

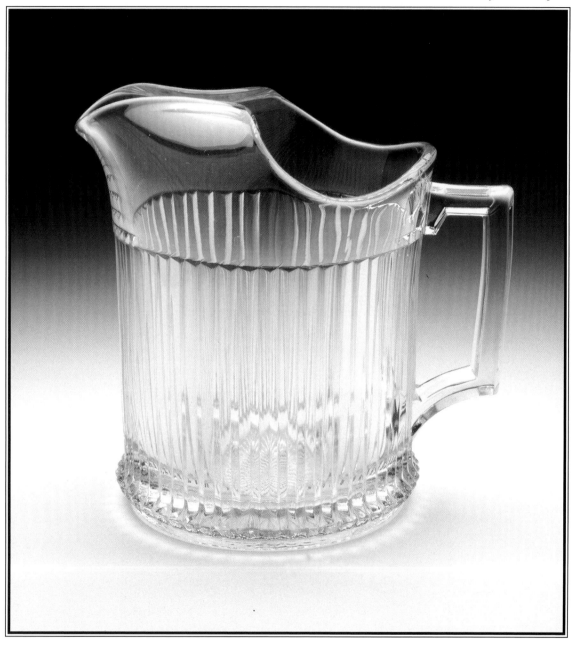

RIDGELEIGH Crystal ½-gal pitcher – rare item

From the collection of Dick and Pat Spencer

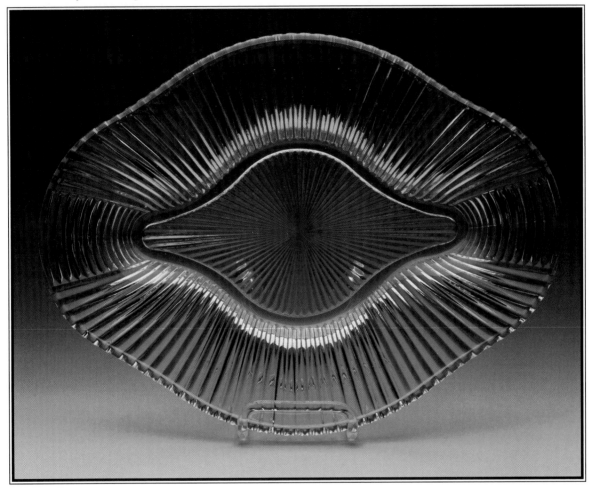

RIDGELEIGH crystal oval hors d'oeuvres plate – rare item
This plate was photographed standing up to better show you the shape.

ROSE crystal 9½" epergne bowl w/epergne vase – rare item

Author's Collection

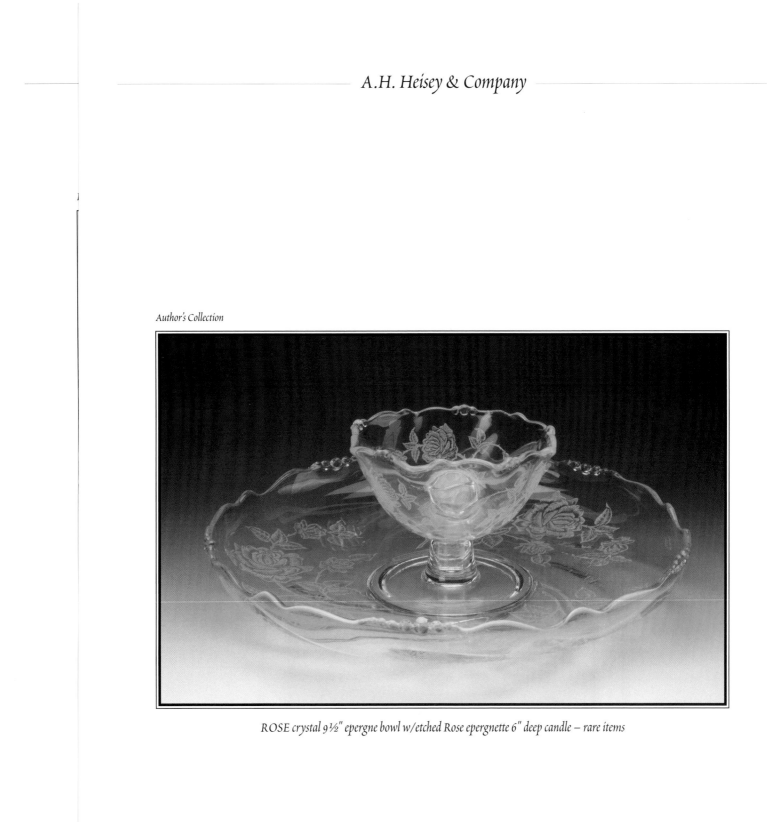

ROSE crystal 9½" epergne bowl w/etched Rose epergnette 6" deep candle – rare items

IMPERIAL GLASS CORPORATION 1904–1984

Although glassmaking began at Imperial in 1904, it was the start of a new era in 1936 when Candlewick was introduced. Until the company's demise in 1984, Imperial turned out a multitude of pieces in this pattern; it was not their only pattern.

CANDLEWICK crystal pitcher w/amethyst foot – rare item

CANDLEWICK caramel slag 400/268, 8″, 2-part relish – rare color

CANDLEWICK crystal 400/245, 6½" candy box – rare item

CANDLEWICK crystal 400/116 ftd. shaker – rare item

Author's Collection

CANDLEWICK *crystal decorated orchid 400/2911 condiment set – rare design*

CANDLEWICK crystal 400/194 domed foot 10" vase – rare item

From the collection of Dan Tucker and Lorrie Kitchen

CANDLEWICK crystal 400/15, 10 oz. tumbler – rare item

From the collection of Dick and Pat Spencer

CAPE COD crystal 160/72, 13″ birthday cake plate – rare item
This cake plate has 72 holes for candles. After 72, you have to buy another cake plate.

CAPE COD iridescent cruet w/stopper – rare color

INDIANA GLASS COMPANY 1907 to Present

Indiana Glass has caused concern for collectors for years with their "reissues." A more proper term might be reproductions! It is a shame because many pieces of their glass fit the rare category.

NO. 622 "PRETZEL" Terrace Green cup – rare color
I can account for three cups in this rare color, but has anyone found a saucer?

Author's Collection

TEA ROOM crystal flat banana split – rare item
Two views are shown so you can ascertain the shape more easily.

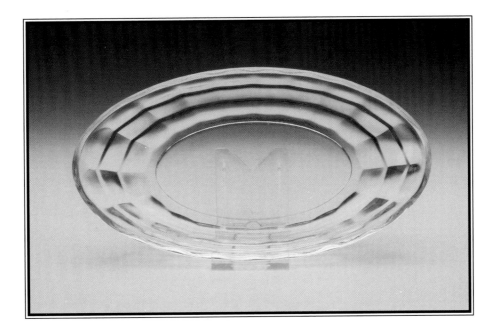

JEANNETTE GLASS COMPANY

Jeannette Glass Company seemed to have an affinity for making odd-colored glass from their standard glassware lines. Canary yellow (vaseline), red, or even Delphite blue turns up in patterns once in a while. What makes this fact even more astounding is that those colors were not part of their repertoire in other patterns either. It's as if they wanted to cause us wonderment years later.

CUBE blue powder jar – rare color
Another shade of blue was pictured in Very Rare Glassware of the Depression Years – fourth edition.

CUBE pink three-footed, 3-part relish – rare item
This relish resides in a Florida collection, but the collector's name has eluded me.

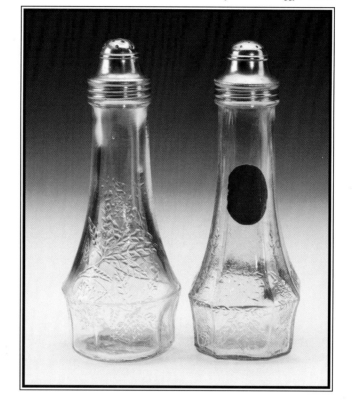

FLORAL pink round bottom shaker – rare item
The round shaker is shown next to the regularly found one for comparison. The bottom photo shows the distinct base shapes.

From the collection of Bill and Lottie Porter

FLORAL Cremax butter dish – rare color

IRIS crystal dinner plate – rare item
This unusual plate may have been experimental.

Author's Collection

IRIS crystal Corsage decoration – rare decoration
Decoration has to be mint for the prices listed!

IRIS iridescent plastic plate – rare item
As with the crystal one found a few years ago, this turned up in the Pittsburgh area.

Author's Collection

SHELL PINK duck powder jar – rare item
Two of these were found several years ago and one was finally placed on the market.

From the collection of Steve Nadort

SUNFLOWER pink 8" salad plate – rare item

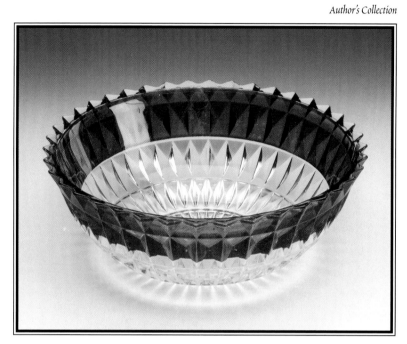

WINDSOR crystal, 8", flashed red, pointed edge bowl – rare decoration

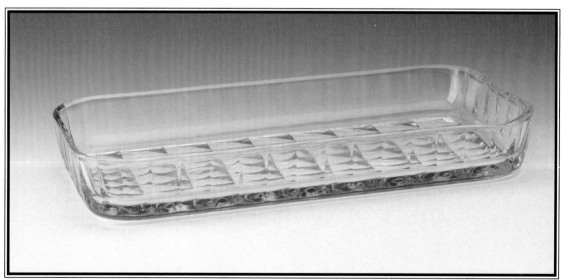

WINDSOR pink 4⅛" x 9" tray w/o handles – rare item

From the collection of Kevin Kiley

WINDSOR *pink 11½", 3-part platter – rare item*

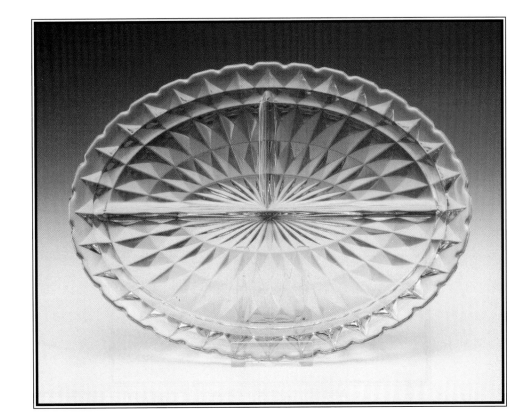

Althouξ
Hocking elin

    Located in New Jersey rather than in the Ohio-Pennsylvania-West Virginia glassmaking triangle, this company prospered during the early days of Depression glass until a fire destroyed the plant which was never rebuilt. They made many utilitarian items and provided us with one of the few dresser sets in pressed ware of the Depression era.

From the collection of Kevin Kiley

AMERICAN PIONEER amber 6½" candlestick – rare color

Alt

MacBETH-EVANS GLASS COMPANY 1899–1937

MacBeth-Evans made some of the more popular Depression glass patterns, but as with competitors' products, some pieces are scarcely found today.

AMERICAN SWEETHEART crystal 4" cream soup – rare item

From the collection of Parke and Joyce Bloyer

AMERICAN SWEETHEART *Monax sugar w/lid (2 styles) – rare item*
The lids are rarely seen, but the one on the right (both top and bottom) is unusual. The normally seen lid is shown for comparison.

The company was originally founded as McKee & Brothers Glass Works at Pittsburgh in 1853. It moved to a site east of Pittsburgh in Westmoreland County in 1888 and built its new plant there. This site became the town of Jeannette. The move from Pittsburgh had been necessitated by the availability of natural gas in the area of Jeannette. Later, with the depletion of this natural gas, the company turned to the other readily available fuel in the area — coal. McKee continued making glass at this site until 1951 when the Thatcher Glass Company bought the company.

When McKee is mentioned today, two things seem to stand out in collector's minds: Rock Crystal and kitchenware items. Collectors of Depression patterns immediately think of the red or crystal Rock Crystal pattern that was made from the early 1900s until the 1940s.

Author's Collection

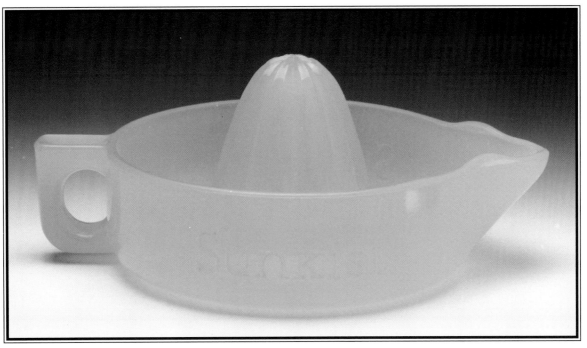

REAMER Clambroth Green Sunkist – rare color

LAUREL French ivory 5" sherbet – rare item

MORGANTOWN GLASS WORKS 1929–1972

First established in Morgantown, West Virginia, as Morgantown Glass Works, it became the Economy Glass Tumbler Co. in the early 1900s until 1929 when it again became Morgantown. It continued as Morgantown until bought out by Bailey Glass in 1972.

Author's Collection

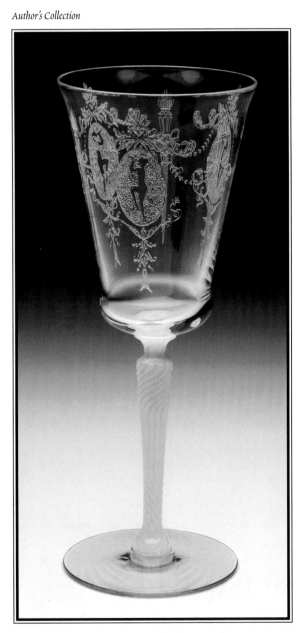

SUNRISE MEDALLION crystal goblet w/opal stem – rare item

NEW MARTINSVILLE GLASS MANUFACTURING COMPANY

1901–1944

Started in 1901, this factory became Viking Glass Company in 1944 and is still in operation today. Although they produced a multitude of colors during the Depression era, New Martinsville exhibited quality color control and were renowned for their Ruby (red) and their Ritz blue (cobalt blue).

JANICE blue 12" basket – rare item

JANICE blue footed, 6" ice tub – rare item

JANICE Emerald Green, footed, 6" ice tub – rare item

MOONDROPS green "rocket" decanter – rare item

Author's Collection

MOONDROPS pink "rocket" 8½" bud vase – rare item

RADIANCE amethyst satinized 10" vase – rare color

RADIANCE black satinized 10" vase – rare color

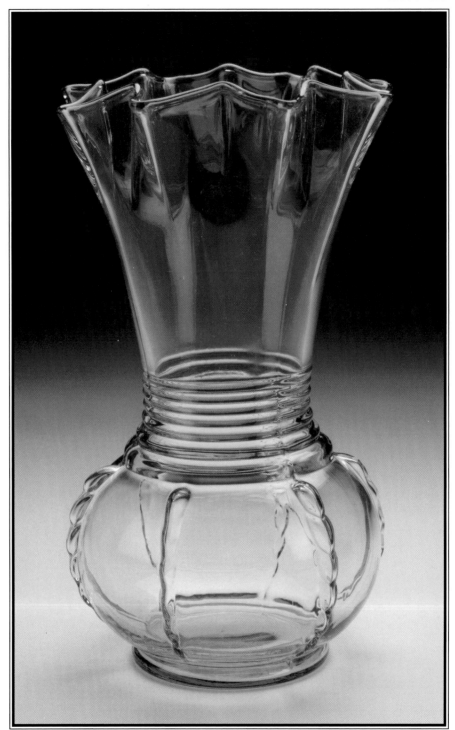

RADIANCE pink 10" vase – rare color

Author's Collection

RADIANCE red 5" ball candleholder – rare item

Author's Collection

RADIANCE red 8" candleholder with boboches attached – rare item
(see next page for different view)

RADIANCE red 8" candleholder with boboches – rare item
Photo redone to illustrate the Radiance pattern on the underside of the boboches.

PADEN CITY GLASS COMPANY 1916–1951

Paden City Glass Company built its factory and started producing glassware all within a one-year period. That was considered quite a feat in 1916. We think of Paden City as a company which produced a multitude of colors and made a variety of patterns containing birds. This handmade glass was not turned out in the large quantities that many of the glass factories of that day produced. Hence, items manufactured by Paden City are even more scarce 50 years later. Most of the glassware made by this company is exceedingly attractive in design.

Author's Collection

CUPID amber, gold decorated, center handled bowl – rare item
This is unusual in that it is found on an Imperial Molly blank.

BLACK FOREST crystal Largo line 220, 10" cracker plate – rare item

From the collection of Bill and Lottie Porter

BLACK FOREST *pink 10½", 72 oz. pitcher – rare item*

GAZEBO blue heart-shaped, 3-part candy – rare item
Two views are shown so you can see pattern and shape of both top and bottom.

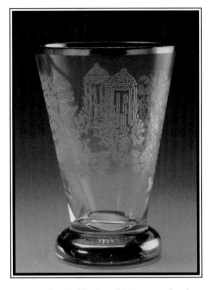

GAZEBO crystal w/gold trim 4" juice or cocktail – rare item

GAZEBO crystal 12", 5-part tray – rare item

ORCHID black 8" vase – rare item

Author's Collection

ORCHID green 10" vase – rare color

ORCHID on red Crow's Foot 6⅝" comport – rare item

From the collection of Paul and Debbie Torsiello

ORCHID red 10″ vase – rare item

Author's Collection

ORCHID red 10″ vase – rare item

Author's Collection

PEACOCK & WILD ROSE *amber satinized 11″ console bowl – rare color*
This bowl is unusual because the pattern is clear and the bowl is satinized.

Author's Collection

PEACOCK & WILD ROSE black 8¼", elliptical vase – rare item

Paden City Glass Company

From the collection of Ted and Judy Johnson

PEACOCK & WILD ROSE pink 8½", 64 oz. pitcher – rare item

161

"PEACOCK REVERSE" black 10" vase – rare item
Pattern has been highlighted for photography purposes.

From the collection of Bill and Lottie Porter

"PEACOCK REVERSE" green 6" round candy dish – rare item

Author's Collection

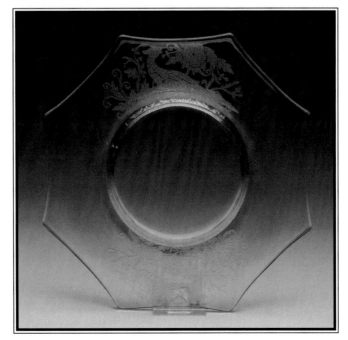

"PEACOCK REVERSE" pink 8½" octagonal plate – rare color and item

TIFFIN GLASS COMPANY
(one of many branches of U.S. Glass)

The "R" factory of the U.S. Glass Company was located at Tiffin, Ohio. It was better known as the Tiffin Glass Company.

KINGS CROWN crystal w/red trim 15-piece punch set – rare set

U.S. GLASS COMPANY 1891–1962

The U. S. Glass Company was founded in 1891 as a merger of 18 smaller companies in Ohio, Pennsylvania, and West Virginia. Tiffin Glass Company was the "R" factory in this merger of smaller companies. While Flower Garden and Butterfly remains the most popular pattern collected from U.S. Glass, other patterns are beginning to attract admirers.

Author's Collection

DEERWOOD pink 10" footed console bowl w/gold trim – rare item
These bowls are usually found in black.

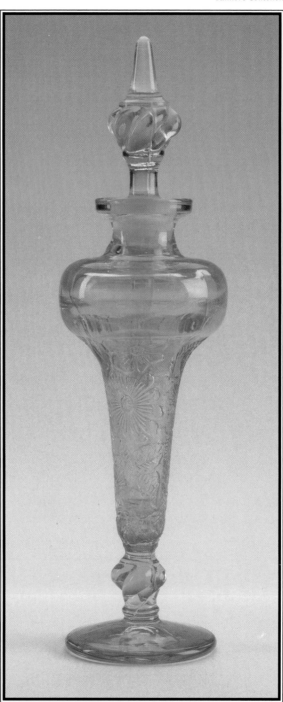

FLOWER GARDEN WITH BUTTERFLIES blue 7½" cologne bottle w/stopper – rare item

Author's Collection

FLOWER GARDEN WITH BUTTERFLIES crystal 7½" cologne bottle w/black stopper – rare color

WESTMORELAND GLASS COMPANY 1890–1983

Started in 1890, in Grapeville, Pennsylvania, as the "Westmoreland Specialty Company," this company is better known by today's collectors for its milk glass productions than many of its numerous other glassware productions.

DELLA ROBIA pink 14" torte plate – rare color
This is the only pink Della Robia piece I have seen.

Author's Collection

PANELED GRAPE green milk glass 6½" vase – rare color

PANELED GRAPE milk glass 12" x 6½" herb planter – rare item
Several of these have turned up recently, so I wonder if they are as rare as they are supposed to be.

Author's Collection

UNKNOWN *black razor hone – rare item*
The back of this blade-edger is marked "Woman's Christian Temperance Union." They must have had some rugged ladies in that group.

VALUE GUIDE

Page 47
CAPRICE Peach Blo 80 oz. ball jug – $1,000.00–1,250.00

Page 48
CHANTILLY crystal #3900/575 10" cornucopia vase – $125.00–150.00

Page 49
CHANTILLY crystal #75 54 oz. pitcher – $175.00–225.00

Page 50
CHANTILLY ebony w/gold decoration #648/119, 6" candelabrum – $250.00–300.00

Page 51
CLEO Willow Blue #813 sugar sifter and #816 ewer creamers – Sugar $500.00–750.00; Creamer $150.00–200.00

Page 52
CLEO Willow Blue #955 62 oz. pitcher – $750.00–1,000.00

Page 53
DIANE amber decanter set – #3400/119 12 oz. Decanter $200.00–250.00; #3400/1344 1 oz. Cordial $80.00–100.00 ea.; # 660 Tray $75.00–100.00

Page 54
DIANE crystal #3011 Statuesque cigarette box – $750.00–1,000.00

Page 55
DIANE gold Krystol #1176 dinner plate – $75.00–90.00

Page 56
ELAINE crystal #3500 6" ram's head candy – $200.00–250.00
ELAINE crystal #485 9½" crescent salad plate – $100.00–125.00

Page 57
ELAINE amethyst frosted goblet – $100.00–125.00

Page 58
ELAINE crystal frosted goblet – $100.00–125.00

Page 59
ELAINE emerald frosted goblet – $100.00–125.00

Page 60
ELAINE Willow Blue #3500/26 12" fruit basket ram's head bowl – $900.00–1,000.00

Page 61
EVERGLADE Carmen 6" double candle w/epergnes – $450.00–500.00

Page 62
GLORIA Crown Tuscan w/gold decoration #1312 footed cigarette box – $200.00–250.00
GLORIA Peach Blo #3130 4⅜" cordial – $135.00–150.00

Page 63
GLORIA gold Krystol 9" #3011 Statuesque comport – $1,250.00–1,500.00

Page 64
GLORIA Willow Blue #3130, 9" comport –$150.00–175.00

Page 65
MT. VERNON Emerald Green (dark) #77 5½", two-handled comport – $75.00–85.00

Page 66
PORTIA Carmen gold encrusted sherbet and sherbet plate – Sherbet $150.00–175.00; Plate $75.00–100.00

Page 67
PORTIA Crown Tuscan w/gold decoration #1237 9" vase – $200.00–225.00

Page 68
PORTIA crystal #170 13" Martha cake plate – $125.00–150.00

Page 69
PORTIA Heatherbloom #3400/1180 5¼" two-handled bonbon – $40.00–50.00

ROSE POINT crystal #1470 ball shaker w/ebony base – $60.00–70.00 ea.
ROSE POINT crystal #3400/77 shakers w/ebony tops – $65.00–75.00
ROSE POINT crystal #498 2 oz. bar tumbler – $100.00–125.00
ROSE POINT crystal #321 2 oz. sham to 1½ oz. bar tumbler – $150.00–175.00

Page 70
ROSE POINT crystal #1055 32 oz. Weiss beer goblet w/gold – $300.00–400.00

Page 71
STATUESQUE #3011 candlestick, Carmen – $400.00–500.00

Page 72
STATUESQUE #3011 cigarette holder, Mocha – $1,000.00–1,200.00

Page 73
STATUESQUE #3011 claret, Smoke Crackle – $400.00–500.00

Page 74
STATUESQUE #3011 comport, Crown Tuscan – $500.00–600.00

Page 75
STATUESQUE #3011 comport, Moonlight Blue – $900.00–1,000.00

Page 76
STATUESQUE #3011 tulip cocktail #3126 emerald – $300.00–400.00

Page 77
WILDFLOWER crystal #119 7" basket – $300.00–350.00

Page 78
WILDFLOWER crystal #1066 oval cigarette holder – $75.00–100.00

Page 79
WILDFLOWER crystal Pristine 575 cornucopia vase – $175.00–200.00

Page 80
WILDFLOWER ebony w/gold decoration #648/119, 6" candelabrum – $250.00–300.00

Page 81
MORGAN pink ice tub – $150.00–200.00

Page 82
MORGAN black w/gold decoration 10" bud vase – $250.00–300.00

Page 83
MORGAN green 10" vase w/ruffled top in holder – Vase $250.00–300.00; Holder $75.00–100.00

Page 84
RUBA ROMBIC black 9" vase – $3,000.00–3,500.00

Page 85
RUBA ROMBIC lilac 3½" ashtray – $800.00–1,000.00
RUBA ROMBIC Smokey Topaz 3" almond – $200.00–250.00

Page 86
RUBA ROMBIC Smokey Topaz 7", 15 oz., ftd. tumbler – $500.00–550.00

Page 87
RUBA ROMBIC Jade 12 oz. flat tumbler – $350.00–400.00

Page 88
CANTERBURY RUBY 10" oval bowl – $100.00–125.00

Page 89
CARIBBEAN blue 6" vase w/frog – Vase $250.00–300.00; Frog $100.00–150.00

Page 90
PATRICIAN amber sugar lid – $150.00–200.00

Page 91
SHARON pink footed vase – one of two known

Page 92
BAROQUE amber 6" three-lite candlestick – $100.00–125.00

Page 141
JANICE Emerald Green, footed, 6" ice tub – $175.00–200.00

Page 142
MOONDROPS green "rocket" decanter – $300.00–350.00

Page 143
MOONDROPS pink "rocket" 8½" bud vase – $175.00–200.00

Page 144
RADIANCE amethyst satinized 10" vase – $125.00–150.00

Page 145
RADIANCE black satinized 10" vase – $150.00–175.00

Page 146
RADIANCE pink 10" vase – $125.00–150.00

Page 147
RADIANCE red 5" ball candleholder – $75.00–100.00

Page 147
RADIANCE red 8" candleholder with boboches attached – $125.00–150.00

Page 148
RADIANCE red 8" candleholder with boboches – $125.00–150.00

Page 149
CUPID amber, gold decorated, center handled bowl – $300.00–350.00

Page 150
BLACK FOREST crystal Largo line 220 10" cracker plate – $40.00–50.00

Page 151
BLACK FOREST pink 10½", 72 oz. pitcher – $450.00–500.00

Page 152
GAZEBO blue, heart shaped, 3-part candy – $200.00–250.00

Page 153
GAZEBO crystal w/gold trim 4" juice or cocktail – $25.00–30.00
GAZEBO crystal 12", 5-part tray – $100.00–125.00

Page 154
ORCHID black 8" vase – $175.00–200.00

Page 155
ORCHID green 10" vase – $100.00–125.00

Page 156
ORCHID on red Crow's Foot 6⅝" comport – $125.00–150.00

Page 157
ORCHID red 10" vase – $175.00–200.00

Page 158
ORCHID red 10" vase – $150.00–175.00

Page 159
PEACOCK & WILD ROSE amber satinized 11" console bowl – $90.00–100.00

Page 160
PEACOCK & WILD ROSE black 8¼", elliptical vase
$350.00–375.00

Page 161
PEACOCK & WILD ROSE pink 8½", 64 oz. pitcher – $400.00–450.00

Page 162
"PEACOCK REVERSE" black 10" vase – $150.00–175.00

Page 163
"PEACOCK REVERSE" green 6" round candy dish – $175.00–200.00
"PEACOCK REVERSE" pink 8½" octagonal plate – $30.00–35.00

Page 164
KINGS CROWN crystal w/red trim 15 piece punch set – $700.00–750.00

Page 165
DEERWOOD pink 10" footed console bowl w/gold trim – $80.00–100.00

Page 166
FLOWER GARDEN WITH BUTTERFLIES blue 7½" cologne bottle w/stopper – $300.00–350.00

Page 167
FLOWER GARDEN WITH BUTTERFLIES crystal 7½" cologne bottle w/black stopper – $300.00–350.00

Page 168
DELLA ROBIA pink 14" torte plate – $100.00–125.00

Page 169
PANELED GRAPE green milk glass 6½" vase – $40.00–50.00

Page 170
PANELED GRAPE milk glass 12" x 6½" herb planter – $100.00–125.00

Page 171
UNKNOWN black razor hone – $50.00–60.00